Good News:

Faith Food Snack Pack

Faith Lifters that Bless and Build Believers

by
Nick Watson

Nick Watson Prophetic Power Ministries
youcanprophesy@gmail.com
www.youcanprophesy.com

Good News:
Faith Food Snack Pack

ISBN 978-0-9943012-3-9

Copyright © by Nick Watson.

All rights reserved. No part of this book may be reproduced or transmitted in any form or by any means, electronic or mechanical, including photocopying and recording or by any information storage and retrieval system, without permission from the author.

Published by Nick Watson Prophetic Power Ministries.

Brisbane. Australia. 4178.

ENDORSEMENTS

Pastor Nick Watson broke new ground with his recent book, "You Can Prophesy – Supernatural. Simple. Safe." The book was straight forward, practical and releasing. His latest book is just as impacting and provides insight and wisdom which if applied will bring release to every person who reads it. As I read the book I was encouraged, inspired and motivated to apply the principles it espouses. I highly recommend you read the book and learn from Pastor Nick's personal understanding of profound scriptural principles.

Wayne Swift

National Leader, Apostolic Church Australia;
Senior Pastor, Church 1330. Scoresby. Victoria. Australia.

Firstly I loved it! – great revelation and content with strong Scriptural foundation and support evidenced right throughout the text. The chapters cover a good diversity of subjects with good use of simple illustrations. I like the application questions and Faith Declarations at the end of each chapter. For me as a preacher, it is certainly a great resource for messages, or preaching thoughts.

Gary Swenson

State Ministries Director,
Australian Christian Churches (previously Assemblies of God) Queensland and Northern Territory

Nick's book is full of great material and reads well. I'd describe it as a wonderful discipleship tool. I enjoy working through this sort of material with my staff team – it grows big people. Well done!!

Sheridyn Rogers

Senior Pastor, Network Leader, Activate churches, NZ

Nick Watson's new book lives up to its name! I found it very inspiring. You will find your faith lifted as you read each chapter. It is clear that he is not simply an author, but he has been a faithful pastor for decades. That pastoral grace comes through as Nick shepherds you into a stronger, more vibrant faith that works in every-day life. Enjoy reading Overcoming Faith Food Snack Pack as a solidly biblical and practical encouragement to strengthen your faith in Christ!

R. Sonny Misar

Author, "Journey to Authenticity". Senior Pastor, Living Light Church. Winona. Minnesota. USA

Nick's book is not only easy to read but one which is practical, has depth and encourages genuine discipleship. This book contains a good mix of Holy Ghost revelation, biblical fact and principles. This book poses simple yet effective principles of discipleship that will open our lives to God's favour and His anointing.

Chris Wickland

Senior Pastor, Living Word Church. Fareham. England.

As a minister of the Gospel for over 35 years I have learned to value good, sound teaching. So it is with pleasure that I recommend Nick Watson's new book. Nick is a seasoned prophet and pastor that understands the battles and trials we face daily and I believe his book will prove a blessing in practical teaching on overcoming these adversities of life.

Dr. Col Stringer

Author of 20 Christian books, President International Convention of Faith Ministers, Australia.

This book is a Biblical gold mine; written to inform truthfully and experientially its readers with life-changing Biblical principles for an exciting, fruitful, loving obedient, Christ-filled "Life!" Throughout the reading of this easy, comfortable, yet exciting writing style of Nick's, he keeps me turning the pages until I become time and again overcome by the wealth of confirmation and witness in my spirit of the treasure truths that are so beneficially needed in our lives at all times.

Rosemary Renninson

International Devotional Writer/Speaker. Moe. Vic. Australia

This is a book I enjoyed and will refer to again and again. For many years I have studied and taught pastoral ministry and done my best to be a good practitioner. This book would have been so helpful! Nick get this published and I will do my best to get it into as many hands I can.

Philip Underwood

Previously National Leader, Apostolic Churches, New Zealand; Senior Pastor (ret.) Cornerstone Church, Philadelphia. PA. USA

FOREWORD

Reading through this book, my heart rejoiced in the wisdom that came through the pages. This is a book of wisdom – and a gift to all believers, but particularly for those called to ministry. And I believe the Holy Spirit has inspired Nick to write this as an inheritance for the next generation of believers.

With many wonderful quotes and anecdotes, Nick imparts to us the blessing of many lessons learned through his years of ministry experience. There are many keys to be discovered by the reader about how to walk in wisdom. Prompting us with revelations and thought provoking stories, Nick has given us a gift that releases hope and help that, if applied, will cause you to walk in greater wisdom and favour.

One chapter had me "Amen-ing" aloud. Take time to absorb and apply the wonderful truths Nick has to share and you will be better for it!

Katherine Ruonala

Author of "Living in the Miraculous: How God's love is Expressed through the Supernatural"
Senior Leader of Glory City Church Brisbane and Apostolic oversight of the the International Glory City Church Network.
Founder and Facilitator of the Australian Prophetic Council.
www.katherineruonala.com

DEDICATION

My three dedications of this book are:

- To the Lord Who has partnered with me in many ways to write it.

- To my wife Lynne and our family of four generations.

- To the people who have encouraged me in ministry, so that I can pay-it-forward.

ACKNOWLEDGEMENTS

I thank my amazing wife and the love of my life, Lynne, for being my indispensable partner in life and in ministry.

My thanks also go to all those who have helped me put this book together. Firstly, my chief editor John MacFarlane without whose skills and efforts this book would not have come into reality. Secondly, my proof-reading family and friends Pastor Robert Couper, Elizabeth Scrimshaw, Barbara Hodgman, Lynne Watson and Bronwyn Cunningham.

Special mention and gratitude goes to Lisa Watson of the Printing Well, Wynnum for her sensational design of my book covers and other printing help she donated towards this project. ***www.theprintingwell.com.au/***

AUTHOR'S CHOICE

I have made two non-traditional choices in this book. Firstly, I have deleted the definite article "the" from the Name of Holy Spirit, because I want Him to become more personal to my readers. Secondly, I have capitalised a lot of pronouns (such as "Him"), in order to give the Lord the honour He is due and to make clear Who the pronoun represents.

BIBLE QUOTATIONS

Unless stated otherwise, all Bible quotations in this book are taken from:

The Holy Bible, New International Version®, NIV® Copyright © 1973, 1978, 1984, 2011 by Biblica, Inc.® Used by permission. All rights reserved worldwide.

Other versions quoted:

King James Version. Public Domain.

The Amplified Bible. Zondervan Bible Publishers. © 1965. 24th reprinting – April, 1982

Scripture quotations marked ESV are from *The Holy Bible, English Standard Version*® (ESV®), copyright © 2001 by Crossway, a publishing ministry of Good News Publishers. Used by permission. All rights reserved.

Scriptures marked ISV are taken from the *Holy Bible: International Standard Version*®. Copyright © 1996-forever by The ISV Foundation. ALL RIGHTS RESERVED INTERNATIONALLY. Used by permission.

The Jerusalem Bible. DARTON, LONGMAN and TODD Ltd. And Doubleday and Company. London. 1968.

The Holy Bible, New Living Translation, copyright ©1996, 2004, 2007 by Tyndale House Foundation. Used by permission of Tyndale House Publishers, Inc., Carol Stream, Illinois 60188. All rights reserved.

The Living Bible copyright © 1971 by Tyndale House Foundation. Used by permission of Tyndale House Publishers Inc., Carol Stream, Illinois 60188. All rights reserved.

New American Standard Bible®, Copyright © 1960, 1962, 1963, 1968, 1971, 1972, 1973, 1975, 1977, 1995 by The Lockman Foundation Used by permission." (www.Lockman.org)

New King James Version®. Copyright © 1982 by Thomas Nelson, Inc. Used by permission. All rights reserved."

Weymouth New Testament in Modern Speech. Third Edition 1913. (Public Domain).

Contents

Chapter 1 – Defeating the Disappointment Spiral 15

Chapter 2 – Praising our Covenant-Keeping Lord 21

Chapter 3 – The Lord's Banner Over You 31

Chapter 4 – Being Led by Holy Spirit 37

Chapter 5 – Forgiveness and Healing in Psalm 103:1-3 47

Chapter 6 – Freedom from Depression, Satisfaction and Renewal in Psalm 103:1-5 61

Chapter 7 – 5 Steps to Forgiving Others 75

Chapter 8 – 5 More Steps to Forgiving Others 87

Chapter 9 – What Jesus did at Easter 99

INTRODUCTION

This mini-book is one of four taken from my book "Lessons from my Dog: 33 Faith-Lifters to bless and build believers." Each mini-book is a topical collection of life-transforming and equipping messages that cover a variety of subjects.

These are Holy Spirit inspired revelations, Biblical teachings, testimonies and illustrations that have proven fruitful in the lives of many people during my years as Senior Pastor of a thriving Spirit-filled, Apostolic church and travelling prophetic minister.

They will help you develop your God-given potential in Christ and equip you to fulfil your ministry that the Lord has assigned to you, by doing the good works of love and faith that He prepared in advance for you to do. (Ephesians 2:10).

I am honoured by the affirming comments of my **anointed, experienced and internationally significant endorsers. Their reviews have confirmed to me that these books are going to meet needs, change lives, multiply ministry, equip believers and fulfil the purposes that the Lord entrusted to me when He anointed me as an author.**

1 *Defeating the* **Disappointment Spiral**

And hope does not disappoint us, because God has poured out His love into our hearts by the Holy Spirit, whom He has given us.

Romans 5:5

In 1858, the Democrat-controlled Illinois legislature sent Stephen Douglas to the US Senate. They had benefitted from a gerrymandered electorate that enabled them to overrule the fact that Abraham Lincoln had won the popular vote. A friend asked Lincoln how he felt. The answer, given by the man who lost virtually every election he contested until he became possibly the greatest President in the history of that great nation, was this: "Like the boy who stubbed his toe, I am too big to cry and too badly hurt to laugh." (Source unknown).

Disappointment is something that affects every person on the planet. Some handle it better than others. If someone does not treat the disappointment in a correct and timely manner, it can become like a small injury that gets infected. The infected area will get worse still and eventually become a serious health issue if remedial action is not taken.

If you will pardon me being a little graphic in my description, I have told many people that it is better to deal with problems at the pimple stage, not the cancer stage.

Deal with problems at the pimple stage, not the cancer stage

The Disappointment Spiral shows how negative attitudes that are not attended to get worse, not better:

(i) Disappointment
(ii) Discouragement
(iii) Disillusionment
(iv) Distorted perspective
(v) Depression
(vi) Distance
(vii) Distrust
(viii) Disbelief
(ix) Deception
(x) Disobedience
(xi) Despair

(xii) Defeat

(xiii) Death, perhaps of a marriage, a career, a ministry or a dream. Sadly, in some instances, the disappointment spiral has ended in suicide.

Did you notice how many words beginning with "dis" are in that downward spiral?

One of the dictionary definitions of "dis", taken from Roman mythology, is the ruler of the underworld. This is a reminder that Satan is either the source or the exaggerator of all the "dis" we suffer from. We must resist him in the Name of Jesus, so that he does not rob us of our blessings and inheritances as the children of God.

Our enemies are not Philistines, like Israel fought in the Old Testament. The New Testament tells us that our enemies are not "flesh and blood" individuals. Our enemies do include negative attitudes, thoughts and emotions in our mind and, as Ephesians 6:12 says, "rulers ... authorities ... powers of this dark world and ... spiritual forces of evil in the heavenly realms".

These enemies cause us to slip down the Disappointment Spiral. They have lots of names, such as dis-ease, dis-unity, dis-comfort, dis-grace, dis-tress, dis-may, dis-respect, dis-aster, as well as all thirteen problems listed in the Spiral itself, and many other things that put downward pressure on our lives.

I want to tell you that our God specialises in releasing uplifting power. He is the wind beneath our wings. (Isaiah 40:31).

Our God specialises in releasing uplifting power. He is the wind beneath our wings.

He can lift us from the bottom to the top and way over that. Remember, Jesus Himself acknowledged that there is a devil who tries his hardest to ruin our lives; but Jesus also said: "I have come that they might have life more abundantly, life to the full, life till it overflows, rich and satisfying life." (John 10:10 various versions).

The Lord doesn't lift us up without our faith and participation. When you are on the spiral, you must want to get off it. You must be willing to use your faith to climb back up that spiral, in the same way the prophet Elijah did.

In 1 Kings 19, Elijah suffered an attack of suicidal depression because of the threat on his life by the evil Queen Jezebel. He walked forty days and nights to the cave on Mount Horeb. Elijah met God there. The Lord asked: "What are you doing here, Elijah?"

(verse 9).This tells us that Christians do not belong on the Disappointment Spiral.

Then the Lord said to Elijah: "Go back the way you came ...". (verse 15). In other words, we need to put our faith to work with the Lord, and any of His helpers, so that we get off the Disappointment Spiral and get flying with eagles as Isaiah 40:31 tells us we can.

What is one thing you have learned from this teaching?

_____

What is one thing you can do to implement this teaching?

_____

Faith Declaration:

I thank You Lord that You are truly the wind beneath my wings. You are my glory and the lifter of my head. You are the One Who enables me to walk with my head held high. I thank You that I can and will, by faith, step into the abundant life Jesus purchased for me. I renounce every work of the devil that has affected my life, in Jesus' Name. I resist every negative force, thought and emotion that has been pushing me onto the Disappointment Spiral. I forgive every person who has impacted my life for worse, not better. I put my faith into action to rise higher than I ever have before. Amen.

2 *Praising our* Covenant-Keeping Lord

When God introduced Himself to Moses at the burning bush, He called Himself "I AM". This tells us several things about the Lord.

Firstly, He is God, the only self-existent, eternal being. He is the Un-caused Cause of the Universe and all in it. He always was, is and forever will be.

Secondly, the Lord is always in the present moment and He is present in the present moment as God.

Thirdly, because God did not qualify His Lordship in any way, it indicates He is Lord in every way. Hallelujah. In other words we can assure the sinner, that God says to them: "I AM your forgiving Saviour." To the sick, He says: "I AM your Healer." To the poor, God says: "I AM your Provider." To the stressed and depressed, the Lord says: "I AM your Peace." In the practicality of your need, in your time of need, God, The Lord is all you need.

God, the Lord, is your wisdom, strength, righteousness and victory. He is your Shepherd, Helper, Teacher, Guide and Empowerer. The Lord your God is all you need to succeed!

Over a period of time, this Name became to be known as Jehovah. At various times The Lord revealed Himself in ways that described His Nature and Divine attributes. His original Name became linked to other descriptive Names. There are eight commonly known redemptive, or covenant, Names of God, Who revealed Himself as I AM, YHWH, Jehovah.

The eight Names are Jehovah Tsidkenu; Jehovah Mkaddesh; Jehovah Roi; Jehovah Shalom; Jehovah Shammah; Jehovah Rapha; Jehovah Jireh; Jehovah Nissi. Using those Names in prayer and praise is one of my favourite ways to express my love for, adoration to and faith in my Lord. Below are some ideas on how you can do the same.

(xiv)   Jehovah Tsidkenu

God, I praise You for being the Lord our righteousness. I praise You Father, because You are righteous and You always do what is right. I thank You for giving me the righteousness of God through Jesus my Saviour.

(xv) Jehovah M'Keddesh

God, I praise You for being the Lord Who sanctifies. I thank You that, when I became born-again in Christ Jesus, You empowered me, by Your Holy Spirit, to live a holy and productive life, which is pleasing unto the Lord and honours God. I thank You, Holy Spirit, because You enable me to overcome the sin, negativity and bad habits in my life and You equip me to serve the Lord by serving people, as a vessel of honour, fit for the Master's use and ready for my God-given destiny.

(xvi) Jehovah Roi

God, I praise You for being the Lord My Shepherd.

I thank You, Father, for making all the promises in the Bible, including those in Psalm 23, belong to me because I have accepted and submitted to Jesus Christ, Your chief Shepherd, as my Lord. Therefore, I thank You that I shall not want, because Goodness and Mercy shall follow me all the days of my life. I am grateful to know that as my good Shepherd, You will always take care of me and make me a healthy, happy and productive member of Your flock.

(xvii) Jehovah Shalom

God, I praise You for being the Lord our Peace. I praise You because You bring peace to troubled souls, relationships and situations. I am grateful that You impart Your Peace to me, even in illogical situations, because I choose to put my focus on and trust in You.

I thank You because Your peace affects every area of my life. By faith in the sacrifice and triumph of Jesus, I have peace with God, within myself, in my body, in my relationships and partnerships, in my finances, in my circumstances and in my ministry. I praise You for the peace I have knowing that You are watching over me, protecting me and all that is dear to me.

I thank You Lord for the fact that, when I cast my cares on You, as I do now, in Jesus' Name, You carry them for me and from me, because You care for me. I trust You to take care of me and of everyone and everything that I care about.

I honour You as the God of peace and believe that You will soon crush Satan under my feet. Lord, by faith, I receive Your peace afresh today.

(xviii) Jehovah Shammah

God, I praise You for being Emmanuel, the Lord Who is always present with me, anywhere, everywhere, all

Praising our Covenant Keeping Lord

the time. I thank You that You are with me always, as the greatest One, in Whom there is all power and authority in Heaven and on Earth. I thank You Lord, because You are a faithful, Heavenly Father to me. No matter what situation I am in, You are always there for me, You always come through for me and You always work all things together for my ultimate good.

I thank You Lord because You are for me, so who can be against me? It's a source of great comfort and confidence to me to know that You are on my side and by my side. Therefore, I will not fear bad news, nor what man or the devil may attempt to do to me and mine. Lord, I believe that nothing is going to happen to me that You and I together can't handle.

I praise You Lord because Your presence with me empowers me to do Your work and will on earth, which blesses people and glorifies You.

(xix)   Jehovah Rapha

God, I praise You for being the Lord our Healer. I thank You Father that You are the Lord Who heals me and Who enables me to live my life in Your health. Thank You Lord, for Your desire that I should prosper and be in health, according to the measure of my prosperity in my spiritual and inner life.

I thank You Jesus for bearing my sicknesses, diseases, pains, afflictions, griefs and sorrows on the Cross. By Your wounds I am healed, both in my inner man and in my physical body. Thank You Lord, for paying the price for my total well-being.

I thank You Holy Spirit for living within my body and for releasing God's healing power within me, according to my needs and my faith. Thank You for giving me Your Word which is life and health to my whole body and Your joy within me which does me good like a medicine.

I thank You Lord for equipping me as a believer in Christ and choosing to use me in the ministry of healing. I praise You because the Bible says that when I lay hands on the sick, believing, in Your Name, then they shall recover. Thank You for giving me Your authority and anointing me with Your Power to heal, for the Glory of God.

(xx) Jehovah Jireh

God I praise You for being the Lord Who will see to it, Whose provision shall be supplied and seen. I thank You Father that You have committed Yourself to supplying all that is needed, both practical and spiritual, for my life, my family, my ministry and my Church, according to Your abundant riches in glory in Christ Jesus. I honour and appreciate You, Lord, as the God of plenty, the One Who is more-than-enough for my every need, desire and opportunity. You are the absolutely reliable and infinitely inexhaustible Source of every good thing in my life.

I bless You because You are so rich, so kind and so generous. I thank You for Your unmerited favour towards me which is evident, because in and through Christ You have granted me all things pertaining to life and godliness, including every spiritual and practical blessing, so that I have an abundance for every good work.

I praise You because You give me the power to make wealth. Therefore, I claim and declare that whatever I put my hand to do shall prosper, as I live in and serve You by faith.

I thank You Lord for allowing me to prove Your faithfulness and generosity by the giving of my freewill offerings and my tithes, which belong to You, to my local Church. I thank You for opening the windows of Heaven over me and mine, and pouring out Your blessing upon us so freely, according to our obedience, love and faith in giving.

I thank You for rebuking the devourer of our finances so that we do not lack for any good thing. I declare in Jesus' Name that there is no recession in the Kingdom of God and that therefore, by faith, we will not live in lack, but in both the sufficiency and abundance of Your supply.

(xxi) Jehovah Nissi

God I praise You for being the Lord my Banner. I thank You Lord that Your banner over me proclaims Your love and victory over my life. I praise You, because Your Love for me is constant and unfailing. I am grateful Lord that You loved me first and You love me faithfully. I love you in return.

I praise You Lord God Almighty, because You have limitless power and strength. You are my help, my strength and my shield. You are the Lord, the All-Sufficient One. You make the impossible become possible to anyone and everyone who believes in You and Your Word. There is nothing and no-one that is too hard for You. You are the God of miracles, Who is always ready, willing and able to do exceedingly abundantly more than all that I can ask or think. Lord, You are the greatest of the great and the best of the best forever.

I rejoice in You, because I am born again, born to win, because my battles are Your battles and victory belongs to the Lord. I thank You for equipping me in Christ to be more than a conqueror. I praise You, because Your Holy Spirit always leads me into victory, by giving me the ability, strategy and opportunity to win, against all odds, in every situation, by faith, to the glory of God. Thank You

Lord for enabling me to possess my promised land, fulfil my potential and destiny, and lead others into victory, for Your Glory's sake.

I conclude this chapter with a faith challenge for you: Faith is not like a single rock that is either big or large. Faith is like a forest, a group of trees. Some trees can be very young or weak and small. Other trees can be so strong, deep-rooted, solid and so full of life that no storm of wind, rain or fire can stop them from producing fruit and new life.

Your faith is probably strong in terms of some of the Names of the Lord I have shared here, but weak when applied to one or more of the other aspects of the Lord's covenant partnership in your life.

My challenge to you is develop your faith in all areas of God's covenant revelation. Build your faith until you believe equally that God is your Righteousness (you are saved because you have received the righteousness of Christ by faith), your Sanctification (He helps you to live a holy life), your Shepherd, your Peace, your Companion (Who is with you always, everywhere), your Healer, your Provider, your Victory and the Lover of your soul.

What is one thing you have learned from this teaching?

What is one thing you can do to implement this teaching?

Faith Declaration:

I thank You Lord for being the faithful covenant-keeping Lord Who has all power to fulfil Your promises. I praise You because You are not a man who would lie or change Your mind. I exalt You, because You watch over Your Word to perform it. I am so grateful that I am never alone in relationship or partnership because You are always with me in all Your covenant abilities. Amen.

3
The Lord's Banner Over You

Moses built an altar and called it The Lord is my Banner.
Exodus 17:15

Too many people have been "labelled" by negativity spoken over them by other people in their lives.

Some time ago, Holy Spirit gave me a memorable visual impression of what the banner of the Lord means to His New Testament people.

There are two meanings.

The first is the one found in Exodus chapter 17:8-16. It is the account of Joshua's victory over the Amalekites on the battlefield at Rephidim. Whenever Moses held up his hands in prayer, Joshua would win the battle. When Moses' hands drooped down, the Amalekites would surge again and the battle would turn in their favour. What a lesson about the power of prayer.

The rod Moses was holding up was spiritually important. It is referred to in Scripture as the rod of

God (Exodus 4:20). In those days it would have had inscribed on it the Name of the Lord, some family names and history, and probably some promises of God or quotes from their history with God. The point is that raising the staff represents lifting up the Name and Word of God in prayer.

When you read the Bible's description of this great victory, you also see the power of partnership in both prayer and action. Aaron and Hur helped the tiring Moses keep his hands in the air. Moses, Aaron and Hur helped Joshua win the battle and Joshua made the prayers become a reality.

Prayer is important; but prayer alone is not enough. Prayer must be accompanied by action. (James 2:17).

Holy Spirit showed me something special about this Old Testament victory. Moses was given the revelation of the Covenant-Keeping God as Jehovah Nissi - The Lord our Banner. He showed me that over me and every believer is an invisible spiritual banner that every invisible spiritual being can see. It says: "Nick (or, in your case, whatever your name is) is a Winner. Signed, God."

The Banner of the Lord over you says: You are a Winner. Signed, God

The second meaning of the Lord our Banner is found in the Song of Solomon.

... his banner over me is love.
Song of Solomon 2:4 ISV

Holy Spirit revealed to me that on the other side of the spiritual banner that God has placed over every believer are the words "I love Nick (or, in your case, whatever your name is). Signed, God."

The Banner of the Lord over you says: I love you. Signed, God

---

This is true of every Christian, and in fact of every human who has ever lived. It was this love that motivated God to send His Only Son, Jesus, to the Cross for each and every one of us.

Of course, just as in normal relationships, it is up to every individual to respond to the love that is shown to them. I said "yes" to God's love by putting my trust in Jesus Christ as my Lord and Saviour. Have you?

You can do so by praying this prayer:

Lord God All-Mighty, I thank You for loving me. I thank You for sending Jesus to pay the price for my sins. I confess my sins and ask Your forgiveness for them. I ask Jesus to come into my life as Saviour and

Lord. I receive my salvation by faith in the Lord and in Your Word. I commit myself to follow Jesus and obey Your Word for the rest of my life. Amen.

What is one thing you have learned from this teaching?

_____

What is one thing you can do to implement this teaching?

_____

Faith Declaration:

I thank You Father God for loving me so much that You sent Jesus to suffer, die and triumph over death and Satan, so I could have a good life on earth and throughout eternity with You. I praise You for putting a spiritual banner over my head that says I am a winner. I declare that I shall win in life's challenges, tests and battles because You are with me and for me as I walk with You. I rejoice in the fact that You love me always, not based on my performance, but purely by Your grace. Thank You for loving me first, faithfully and eternally. Lord, I love You in return.

Good News: Faith Food Snack Pack

Being Led by **Holy Spirit**

For all who are being led by the Spirit of God, these are sons of God.
Romans 8:14 NAS

In this chapter I am sharing with you some principles I have learned over the years as I have developed my own walk with the Lord, my own capacity to hear His voice and the prophetic ministry He has given me.

(i) Read your Bible

If you want to hear from God, read your Bible, which was written by Holy Spirit through various servants of God.

Once, while I was reading Ezekiel 12:3 KJV, the Lord told Lynne and me to "remove thy stuff". To us at that time, it meant: "Take your old furniture with you to Brisbane." We had not intended to do that. We were going to buy new furniture when I got a job there. I didn't ever get a secular job in our new city. I was basically full-time in ministry from the day we arrived. We didn't get a full salary for two years. We could not have afforded to buy new furniture. God knew that in advance of our moving interstate.

A number of years ago, God spoke to me through Job 8:5-7 NIV with a message that directed my decision making. Those verses told me what was going to be the course of my life for years to come, starting with a restoration of my ministry as Senior Pastor of Bayside Christian Family (Apostolic) Church.

On the night my dad died, I cried out to God to show me if dad was eternally safe. I turned to my evening Bible reading and straightaway came to Psalm 61:7 KJV. "He shall abide before God forever." Peace flooded my soul. Two friends sang those verses at dad's funeral.

(ii)   **Be a good son of God.**
If you want to hear from God, treat Him with respect. Be a good sheep, not a stubborn, rebellious, do-your-own-thing goat. Tell God as Jesus did: Not my will but Yours be done. Be a good son, not a lazy, selfish, give-it-to-me-now teenager. Yield your spirit, soul and body to Him, as described in Romans 12:1-2 and 6:13. Then, ask the Lord to lead you and reveal His wisdom to you. (James 1:5-8).

(iii)   **Believe for the ministry gifts of Holy Spirit**

Earnestly desire spiritual gifts, both for yourself and to hear from God through mature, anointed Christians, who are experienced in operating such gifts, especially prophecy. (1 Corinthians 12:31 and 14:1).

(iv)   **Ask God questions.**

Practice prayer journaling and expect God to answer you, because prayer is a two-way conversation of worship, intercession and listening, not a one-way dump-all-your-troubles-on-God session. You can and should ask the Lord questions about your own life and about people He wants you to minister to.

(v)   **Understand God is sovereign about what and when He speaks.**

Be aware that God doesn't say more than He has to or speak as often as we might like Him to. Sometimes He is like the voice on your GPS, which tests your faith in its previously given directions by times of silence.

(vi)   **Obey what God last revealed to you.**

If you want to hear the next thing God has in mind to say, first obey the last thing He said.

(vii) Learn to discern between the three inner voices you hear.

It would be easy if God spoke like Texan, the devil or like a mafia don or any voice so different from your own that you could immediately tell which voice was God, which was self and which was the evil one.

The problem stems from the fact that we are created as a tripartite being of spirit, soul and body, just like God, the three-in-one Divine Trinity. God speaks to us like deep calling to deep, as the Psalmist wrote. (Psalm 42:7a). He is Spirit and He speaks to our spirit. The devil is also a spirit-being. He too speaks to our spirit.

When these two spirit-communications are given to us, they have to be transferred into our soul in order for us to comprehend them. Sadly, when they arrive in our soul, they have lost their distinct "accent". They sound and feel just like our own thoughts.

Through intimacy of relationship with the Lord and knowledge of His Word, we learn which is the Voice of God and which is the devil and which is just us.

Developing your intimacy with the Lord and your knowledge of His Word equips you to discern God's Voice

The content and impact of the message is a good guide to its source. If it's positive and biblical, it's probably God. If it's negative and produces bad feelings inside you like fear or anger or jealousy, then it's going to be the devil.

If it's you and it's positive, step out in faith anyway. If it's you and it's negative, ignore it. Rather, focus on the positive things of the Word, such as Paul advised in Philippians 4:8.

The positive or negative content and impact of the inner message is a key to discerning its source.

18 ways that God speaks

In my book, *You Can Prophesy – Supernatural. Simple. Safe.* I included a chapter listing 18 ways in which God speaks.

(1) The Quickened Word from the Bible. Many will understand this as receiving a "rhema" from the "logos".

(2)   Journaling.

(3)   The Still Small Voice, which means thoughts and words that come into your mind, which may be quite faint. 1 Kings 19:12. The "still, small voice" is probably the most usual method the Lord uses in communicating with mature ministers.

(4)   The Audible Voice of God.

(5)   A Dominant, Persistent, Repetitive word, thought or phrase that comes into your mind.

(6)   An Inner Witness, an impression, which can be fleeting words, feelings or pictures in your mind.

(7)   An Inner Picture that you "see" in your spirit without actually seeing it in your mind.

(8)   Conviction, an inner "knowing", that mostly builds within you over time.

(9)   Spontaneous revelation, an inspired piece of God's knowledge or understanding.

(10)   Vision. This is a clear picture or a video clip that you see with your eyes or in your mind while you are awake. Unless the meaning is very obvious, the vision will require an interpretation, which Holy Spirit will either give to you or to someone else as you share it.

(11)   Dream.

(12)   Visitation of the Lord or of an angel.

(13) Heavenly revelation. More people than ever before are testifying of being taken to Heaven in the spirit (not physically). Many receive revelation from the Lord Himself.

(14) Remembrance. Holy Spirit may remind you of something such as a Bible verse, an illustration, a quote or a testimony.

(15) Revelation. This may be sparked by anything that gets your attention, such as a circumstance, an event, a casual remark, a person's name, or by a "thing".

(16) Spiritual gifts.

(17) Spiritual partnership in prophetic ministry. This can be when spiritual gifts go together.

For example: in healing ministry, the Word of Knowledge and the gift of Faith are partners. In prophetic ministry, Tongues and Interpretation are two gifts of Holy Spirit that are designed to be used in tandem. A third example is that during church meetings, Holy Spirit may inspire you through the contribution of another person.

(18) Prophetic Presbytery. This is when two or more prophets operate together in ministry to people.

If you receive a serious revelation, make sure you get it confirmed by others who are spiritually qualified to discern it.

(viii) Circumstances can confirm God's Will

Sometimes God uses circumstances to confirm His will. I often tell people that if they are feeling led to relocate somewhere, first go to that place for a holiday. See how you feel there. If things line up, such as positive new connections being made or doors opening there or closing where you are, then it is likely you are heading in the right direction.

However, circumstances must be only the confirming, not the decisive factor, in discerning God's Will. There was a boat waiting for Jonah to take him away from where God wanted him to be. That circumstance did not express what the Spirit was saying.

(ix) Persistent prayer will enhance discernment between two alternatives

I have found that if you have two alternatives to pray about, the one that is of God will grow the more you pray and the other will fade, or at least lose its attractiveness. The God-choice will become more appealing and will excite either peace or faith, or both, within you.

The two inner signs of peace in your heart and of excitement that is spiritual and accompanied by rising faith, are key indicators of the Spirit's leading you into the Will of God.

(x) God may choose unlikely people to speak to you

From the account of the false prophet Balaam, we learn that God can speak through a donkey. (Numbers 22:21-31). He can speak through your parents, or your teenager. Your critic might get something right and it could be a word from God for you. Sometimes a person makes a statement during a conversation that you recognise as having Divine application to your situation.

Sometimes, you can be the donkey. I have had the experience that as I have counselled someone, God has spoken to me through my own advice to them. On other occasions, I have made what I call a "prophetic blurt". I have said something casual that was like a word from God to the person.

What is one thing you have learned from this teaching?

What is one thing you can do to implement this teaching?

Faith Declaration:

I thank You Lord for giving me Your Holy Spirit as my Teacher, Helper and Guide. I am so grateful that You are a God Who hears, speaks and leads His people. I declare in Jesus' Name that, because I have chosen to walk in God's ways, my steps are being ordered by the Lord. I praise the Lord because I have open access to the Word of God, the Mind of Christ, the Wisdom of God, prophetic gifts and prophetic people. Hallelujah.

5

Forgiveness and Healing
in Psalm 103:1-3

In these few verses of this wonderful Psalm, we see the Good News of the Gospel revealed in the Old Testament in all its glory. We are told to not forget the benefits that come from being a Christian, a believing Christ-follower. They are life-changing, life-enriching benefits. When we are aware of them they stimulate our faith to receive all that God has given to us in Christ and through His suffering, sacrifice and triumph for us.

(i) Receiving the benefits of salvation starts with a whole-hearted relationship with God.

Praise the Lord, my soul; all my innermost being, praise his Holy name.

Psalm 103:1

I want you to notice the word "all", which occurs four times in the first three verses of the Psalm. Praise the Lord, all my innermost being. Then, it says, forget not all His benefits. And then, He forgives all my sins, and He heals all my diseases. Isn't that awesome? Give

God your all and you will get His all. That's what the little word "all" is telling us, starting right here in verse 1.

Give God your all and you will get His all

In Jeremiah 29:13, God says "*you will seek Me and you will find Me when you search for Me with all your heart.*" God is far too important for Him to be an "if", "but", or "maybe" or any kind of low priority in your life.

If you want the benefits of Psalm 103 to come true in your life, you must make a commitment, right at the start, in verse 1. You've got to say: "God, I give you my all." Then you will see all the benefits because they flow out of your relationship with and devotion of all your being to the Lord.

This verse also teaches us to praise God at all times. Never blame Him for bad things that might happen. He is good all the time. All the time, God is good. Praise unlocks the power and blessing of God into your life. This was the key given to the barren and desolate woman in Isaiah 54:1-5. She was promised that if she would praise the Lord and act in faith, she would experience far more good than she could ask or think or imagine.

(ii)   Faith and focus are required to receive all the benefits Jesus has purchased for you.

Praise the Lord, my soul, and forget not all His benefits.

Psalm 103:2

There can be a big stumbling block to people receiving these benefits. Our human minds can be so negative. Negativity depletes our faith. Lack of faith robs us of blessing.

Of course, there are those people who are born optimists. Don't you sometimes want to kick them out of the room? Those people who just radiate confidence. Nothing is too hard for them. They say: "Let's just give it a shot, easy-peasy, no problem whatever." Those kind of people, like over-the-top Pollyannas, can be so annoying.

That's because most of us don't think like that. For many people, when bad things happen to them, even a little pinprick of bad, they focus on that, instead of on the good things they have experienced recently. They remember good things as if they were written in water, but bad things as if they were written in stone. The good things that touch their lives are like a quickly fading shadow. They enjoy the moment, but half an hour later, reality bites again.

If something bad happens, negative-minded people think about it the rest of the day, the rest of the week, the rest of the month, maybe even the rest of the year or worst of all, the rest of their lives. The Psalmist is telling us to do the very opposite of that. We are to remember the benefits that the Lord showers upon His people.

So, right here in verse 2, the Psalmist is talking about an attitude to God, an attitude to the Word, an attitude to life, an attitude about yourself and about the quality of your life. Train your mind, so that instead of thinking about something negative that happened to you, whether it was today or twenty years ago, you choose to forget not all these benefits. Decide to focus on the promises of God's Word.

That positive focus will increase your faith and that faith will prepare you to receive the benefits of the Good News of the Word of God. If you don't have an expectation of any benefit or any good thing happening in your life, it isn't going to happen. If you're not expecting something good, if you're not expecting the good plans of God to come to pass in your life, then they are not likely to happen, are they?

Without faith you can't please God. Without faith, you can't receive a miracle. Without faith, you won't get blessed or experience the benefits of God's Word.

Keep your eyes on God and keep believing His promises, no matter what happens around you. Don't forget all His benefits either by neglect, such as by getting too busy with life to read God's Word, or by focusing on negative things.

(iii) The benefit of being forgiven by God and released from the penalty and power of sin.

Who forgives all your sins, ...
Psalm 103:3a

What better people some would be if they really believed this. Sin holds people in an evil grip. It puts guilt and shame on people. It tells people that they're weak and not strong. Sin is an awful taskmaster. It puts people into such a negative quality of life and can even make them sick.

I remember reading a book by Pastor David Yonggi Cho. He told a story of how this young woman came to him for help. She wasn't eating. She was virtually wasting away. Her life was just a misery. As he began to talk and pray with her, she confessed that there was a time in her life when her older sister and brother-in-law had to bring her into their home. While she was living there her brother-in-law forced himself upon her, without her sister's knowledge. This went on for some time. She became so guilt ridden and ashamed, even though it wasn't her fault. She didn't want it to happen, but her brother-in-law forced the situation, and she was left with the consequences of it. She began to physically waste away, as well as internally be so crippled and negative. Both the Bible and medical science acknowledge that there is a relationship between your health and your mental attitude.

Sin can do to you and your physical health the same type of things that happened to that young woman. Sin lets the devil in. Conversely, when you understand that God forgives all your sins, you will have peace, health and joy in your life.

If the Lord so freely gives us His forgiveness, we cannot disagree with Him. If you hang on to your guilt or shame after you have confessed your sins to Him, you are actually acting as if you have a better sense of justice and grace than God Himself does. That is ridiculously wrong.

Let me show you how wonderful God's forgiveness is: Think of His forgiveness being as big as the biggest and deepest ocean, as infinite as His love. Now imagine you are alone with the Lord on an aircraft carrier out in the middle of that ocean. There is no land in sight. Here you are on this big aircraft carrier with all your sins. The Lord is standing next to you and He says: "Look at this ocean of my forgiveness. What sins have you there? Have you a little sin?" "Yes, I have a little sin. Here it is, Lord." "Okay, throw it overboard." You throw it away.

Where's that sin now? It's at the bottom of the sea of God's forgiveness. What about if you had a middle-sized sin? Maybe it's about the size of a briefcase. You throw it into the ocean. Where does it go? Straight to the bottom of the ocean deep.

Now, have you got a big sin? Maybe you've got a big sin – it's as big as an army tank, it's as big as a house, it's as big as a multi-story building. So, you throw that one in. Whoosh, in it goes. Where is it now? It's at the bottom of the ocean of God's forgiveness, with all the rest of your sins.

It doesn't matter if you've got one, two or three sins, or if you have one, two or three thousand sins, or one, two or three million sins. It doesn't matter how big they are, how small they are, how many they are, how few they are; they all go into that ocean and there's not even a ripple, much less an earthquake or a tsunami.

The Bible says that God chooses to remember our sins no more. It's as if you had never sinned. The Bible actually says in the New Testament, that He blots them out. Now, I don't know about you, but when I was a boy, everything was done by hand. There were no Android tablets, Apple iPhones or personal computers.

If I made a mistake writing out a sentence, the teacher said: "Take a ruler and rule a line through the middle of the incorrect word. Then write the correct word next to it." I didn't like the remembrance of my mistake staring me in the face. So, what I used to do was use my pen to completely overwrite the word until it was rendered illegible, being completely and untidily covered in a dark inky cloud. Therefore, any reader couldn't tell what actual mistake I'd made. Unfortunately, there was now a massive blotch on my page. If I was really ashamed of the mistake I'd made, I'd go to the back of the page and I would put another blotch on the back, so that they couldn't read it backwards, from the underside of the page.

These days Bill Gates and Microsoft have come to the rescue of mistake-makers. They remove all my writing sins as if they'd never existed in the first place. Nobody knows what mistakes I've made before I submit my thesis or put my sermon up on the screen.

Both the Old Testament (Isaiah 43:25) and New Testament (Colossians 2:14) talk about God blotting out our transgressions. He doesn't just remove the sin, but He removes the guilt and the shame and the fear of it happening again.

Jeremiah 31:34 tells us that the Lord chooses to not remember our sin any more. He doesn't have amnesia, He simply chooses to switch off His memory of it. You and I must do the same. We need to think like this: "Okay, I did do that. Lord, I ask Your forgiveness. Now that You have chosen to not remember my sin Lord, I'm going to be like You. I'm going to choose not to remember. And if it ever comes up in my mind again, I will say thank You Lord for your forgiveness. I will again choose not to remember it and I will focus my attention on something else."

Christians must learn to not remember their confessed sins, but at the same time, to forget not all the benefits of their salvation, including what it's like to be forgiven and free of sin.

Remember not your forgiven sins. Forget not all the benefits given to you in the Word of God, because of Jesus

How good it is to be enabled to walk with your head held high (Leviticus 26:13) and to have confidence about who you are in Christ and about your future in Him.

How good it is to not think that the negatives of the past are going to dictate the rest of your life. Hallelujah! How good it is to say: "I've been set free. My life is blessed. I'm expecting good things in my life."

(iv) The benefit of healing, both physical and internal.

Who heals all your diseases
Psalm 103:3b

Healing applies to all our sicknesses and dis-eases. I believe the Bible teaches and expresses right here that healing is part of our salvation package. Just as you can receive your salvation, your passport to heaven by faith, so you can receive your healing by faith. Before, on and after the cross, Jesus purchased for us both forgiveness of our sin and the healing of our body.

That's what happened when the paralysed man was lowered down through the roof by his four friends, in Mark 2:1-12. What was the first thing Jesus said to him? Your sins are forgiven. Have you ever wondered what kind of sins a paralysed man can commit? It's not like he can go and rob a bank, is it? A lot of sins we commit are in our head and our heart. Things such as anger, jealousy, lust and pride. Then, there is our mouth! How many times have we deserved to have it washed out with soap? Probably there were occasions when mum didn't need to threaten it; we knew we deserved it enough to almost do it ourselves. That's especially true on those occasions when we said things we wished we could take back; but sadly we can't. We can only apologise and ask forgiveness from the person and from the Lord.

Jesus said, "your sins are forgiven", and then He said "you're healed". There can be a relationship and a pattern here. First, you get the sin out of your life and then second, the healing will come. However, it is not a rule, because Jesus ministered healings of all different kinds and miracles to so many people. He never once was conditional in releasing their healings. Not once did He ever say: "There is no healing for you. God wants you to be sick." Not once did He ever say: "You've been naughty too often." Not once did He say: "It's not your time to be healed."

Jesus gave absolutely unconditional healing to every person, good or bad, young or old, big problem or small problem. Whatever is your need, come to Jesus for this benefit of the Gospel. He says to you: "Out of the grace that is upon Me, out of the goodness of God that is within Me, out of the power of God that flows through My life, be healed, no questions asked, no conditions."

This is the good news. You've got to expect good news in your life, right now, this year. Say to yourself and before the Lord on His throne of grace: "In Jesus' Name I'm going to be healthy this year, I'm going to be healed this year."

Over the years, I have ministered many prayers of healing and seen a number of memorable healings. One was a girl with a broken leg, who was healed in our Church one Sunday morning. The young girl had some soft bone problems previously in her medical history. She came hurtling round a corner and ran into the friend whom she was chasing, who had stopped suddenly. When she ran into her friend, she broke her leg. That was the medical opinion, both of her mother, who was a nurse, and the mother of the other girl, who was also a nurse. They looked for Dr. Luke, who was a valued member, leader and preacher in our church at that time. He has now planted a church elsewhere in Brisbane. He had already left church that morning, so they asked me to come and pray.

The young girl was so embarrassed, she didn't want me there. She was lying on the ground, with the blood drained from her face and her leg swollen, but not penetrated by the bone. So I prayed a short healing prayer for her and left that area of the church fairly quickly. I can't say to you that I had this incredible miracle working faith. I just did what the Bible said.

Five minutes later I was out having coffee with some other people and the mother and daughter walked out to the car.

On the Tuesday, the young girl got her pain back in her leg. Her mother said, "What happened on Sunday? Jesus healed you, didn't He?" "Yes Mum." "All the pain went didn't it?" "Yes Mum." "And the swelling went down?" "Yes Mum." "So, this is just the devil trying to put it back on you isn't it?" "Yes Mum." "Well, we're not going to let him do that are we?" "No

Mum." "So we're going to tell the devil to get the hell out of your body and our family." They did that and the pain never came back. As I understand it, she has not had a soft bone issue since then.

Whether it's a sickness or an accident or if it's hereditary, there's no limit on what God can do.

What is one thing you have learned from this teaching?

What is one thing you can do to implement this teaching?

Faith Declaration:

I thank You Lord for all the benefits Your Word promises me and Jesus purchased for me. Lord, You gave me Your all and I now declare that I give you my all, not out of compulsion or even my desire to be blessed, but because I love You and that is because You first loved me. I ask You to forgive my sins and wash me clean, blotting out my iniquities. Create in me a pure heart, a right and loyal spirit and a willing attitude, in Jesus' Name. Amen. I declare according to Your Word that I am the righteousness of God in Christ, a saint not a sinner. I thank You for my healing and I command my body to be fully and permanently healed, because by the wounds of Jesus I am healed. I ask You Lord to manifest that healing in my body now, in Jesus' Name. Amen.

6
Freedom from Depression; Satisfaction and Renewal
in Psalm 103:1-5

In the first three verses of this Psalm, as described in the previous chapter, we are told to remember and be grateful for all the benefits of our relationship with God. These benefits start with salvation and the forgiveness of our sins. They include our healing, both internally and physically.

There was a television salesman on Australian television some years ago, whose key marketing phrase, which became a by-word in our nation, was: "But wait; there's more."

Psalm 103 is like that. These first few verses do not describe the full range of benefits of this Psalm. The rest of the Bible adds lots more benefits that are the inheritance of the born-again children of God.

(i) The Lord can lift you out of depression

Who redeems your life from the pit
Psalm 103:4a

I'm not sure that there has ever been a more stressed and/or depressed generation than this generation. We create our own depression by over-spending. Some people are motivated to "keep up with the Jones'". They get into credit card debt which they are unable to pay. Some people in lower socio-economic circumstances see others on television enjoying benefits they don't have and if they can't access more finance or more credit, they either get angry that the financial gap between people is so wide or they get depressed about what they don't have.

Secondly, there is so much, too much, divorce. In previous generations, there wasn't so much divorce. People didn't say: "I'm married until it gets too tough"; or "I'm married until I can't be bothered anymore"; or "I'm married until I find someone else that I'm more interested in". It wasn't like that. Marriage was respected as the covenant that it is. Men and women stuck with the covenant and they worked through their issues.

My wife and I had issues. We were separated 3 times in the first 5 years. Then we found the Lord and discovered all the benefits of loving, believing in, obeying and serving Him. Lynne has kept me in line for another 40 years since then and we are both happy together.

Of course, divorce has serious negative emotional and financial consequences. It is a big contributor to depression in society among men, women and children.

There are also people who over-prioritise their work and live in stress. This is the way society is geared today. Both parents have to go out and work, and they have to work long and hard, in order to keep up with the mortgage, the costs of education and to live a modern lifestyle that includes having an array of expensive gadgets.

But we can have a peace. In Philippians 4:6-7, the Bible says, prayer can produce a peace that passes understanding. A peace that's beyond the logic of our circumstances. A peace that's beyond the logic of what is going on in the world, and beyond the negative things that people are saying. You can have an inner peace.

The Lord can lift you up out of depression. He can lift you up out of fear. He can lift you up out of negativity.

I had a crazy upbringing and it was made worse by the fact that I was born with a tendency towards a pessimistic attitude to life. Over all these years of living with the Lord, my "bent" has changed from leaning the wrong way to standing up and leaning in the Lord's way, the right way, the faith way, the love way, the truth way. The tree of my life has put down roots in God and roots in the Word of God. The Lord has changed me from the inside out. He has produced in me faith and love and wisdom and courage and strength. He has given me what I need to succeed in life and to help others succeed also.

I can tell you that if He can bend my tree, He can bend yours. The Lord can lift you up out of that pit and He can put you in a place of confidence and strength and joy and peace. The Good News of the Gospel and this Psalm is that God wants to do that.

Think about this illustration: Imagine that every person in the world can handle 100 units of stress. There are 2 sources of stress, internal and external. Now, imagine you have 85 units of internal stress? This is created by such things as sin, fear, guilt, shame, depression, unresolved issues, resentments, offences, prejudices, problems with rejection and so many other problems bottled up inside of you. There are 85 of your stress units already filling up your capacity tank. You can only handle 15 stress units from the outside world.

This is why for some people, just a small thing can set off a massive reaction. Why? Not because of the size of the small thing, but because they've got too much internal stress, and they can't handle even a small amount of extra pressure or negativity.

Whereas, for another person who doesn't have all that internal stress, it's just a pinprick. He doesn't even notice it and certainly doesn't worry about it or waste time and energy being angry about it.

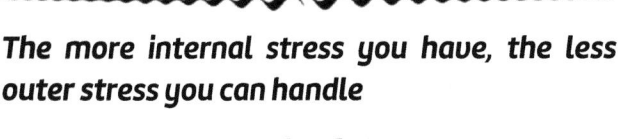

The more internal stress you have, the less outer stress you can handle

If you receive God's love and forgiveness and grace and if you love God and let God truly be Lord of your life and let Him touch you in spirit, soul and body, then your stress units internally will go down. Your peace and courage and strength and faith and love units will go up. You will be able to handle more of the pressure of life even if nothing external changes. You will be able to handle life better. This is what God does for you and with you and in you.

(ii) God doesn't only deal with your negatives, He pours the positives into your life

Who crowns you with love and compassion
Psalm 103:4b

This verse paints the image in me of God being there with you, bringing His infinite supply of everything good to you. He's pouring it out over your life. It's not because you deserve it. It's just that He's got too much. His heart is too full of love and kindness and generosity to keep it all to Himself, so He's got to give it away to anyone who wants what He's got.

It's as if God is saying in these verses: "Look, I've got this never-ending supply that I want to give away. Do you want some? I have more than enough for all.

This is what Grace is. Grace is God doing it out of the goodness of His heart, not because we earn it or deserve it, because we cannot do either. Will you allow God to fill you?

Jesus was often moved by compassion to do miracles. The Lord can do miracles in your life just because He wants to; just because He has compassion for you and your life's circumstances; just because He wants you to have a better life.

When I think about the word "compassion", I also think about this contrast: justice is when we get what we deserve; mercy is when we do not get what we deserve; grace is when we get what we do not deserve.

The problem is that too many people want justice for other people and grace for themselves. You can't do that. You've got to be a person who's willing to express grace towards others, if you want to receive grace, because God gives more grace to the humble. (James 4:6).

Justice is when we get what we deserve. Mercy is when we do not get what we deserve. Grace is when we get what we do not deserve.

(iii) God does more for His people than meet their bare necessities.

Who satisfies your desire with good things
Psalm 103:5a

The first verse of the great shepherd Psalm 23 tells us that when the Lord is our shepherd, we shall not want. That does not mean God keeps His sheep on survival rations. Neither does Jesus' statement about praying for our daily bread in the famous "Our Father" prayer that He taught His disciples. That part of the prayer is symbolic of us asking God to provide all we need to succeed in life and in service for and with Him to bless others.

Our wonderful, loving, kind, rich and generous Father God wants to freely give us every good gift and especially His Holy Spirit. The following verses should convince you and give you faith to believe that God wants to bless you in lots of ways that are above and beyond your survival needs.

> *[9] "Which of you, if your son asks for bread, will give him a stone? [10] Or if he asks for a fish, will give him a snake? [11] If you, then, though you are evil, know how to give good gifts to your children, how much more will your Father in heaven give good gifts to those who ask him!*
>
> *Matthew 7:9-11*

> *"Which of you fathers, if your son asks for a fish, will give him a snake instead? [12] Or if he asks for an egg, will give him a scorpion? [13] If you then, though you are evil, know how to give good gifts to your children, how much more will your Father in heaven give the Holy Spirit to those who ask Him!"*
>
> *Luke 11:11-13*

> *The young lions lack food and suffer hunger, but they who seek (inquire of and require) the Lord [by right of their need and on the authority of His Word], none of them shall lack any beneficial thing.*
>
> *Psalm 34:10 AMP*

> *For the L*ORD *God is our sun and our shield. He gives us grace and glory. The L*ORD *will withhold no good thing from those who do what is right.*
>
> *Psalm 84:11 NLT*

Delight yourself in the Lord and He will grant you the desires of your heart.

Psalm 37:4

It is important for me to highlight here the greatest desire of all. That is the desire to go to Heaven. Everyone wants to go there. Well, God says you can. But if you knock on Heaven's door in your own name, you won't get in. So when I go knocking on Heaven's door, I'm not going to say "Hey God, it's Nick!". What I am going to say is "Hey God, I'm here in the name of Jesus. My name is Nick". And the Lord or His angel will say: "Yeah, sure, come on in."

You can only get into God's Heaven – and remember it's His home and we need His permission to enter there – through Jesus. He is the only door. (John 10:7,9). Jesus is the only way. (John 14:1-6; Acts 4:12). There's no back way. There's no climbing through windows. There's no bribing the door-keeper. There's just one door and Jesus is that door. And Jesus satisfies your desire to go to heaven.

When I was a teenager, I lost the impossible-to-lose job. I went out gambling and partying of a night and turned up to work late and had too many days off. My own immaturity and stupidity cost me dearly. Around that time I felt purposeless. I remember asking myself: "What am I meant to do with my life?" I thought: "Maybe I'm on earth to do something bad, like blow up a bank." I don't know why I thought of blowing up a bank; but that's what I thought. Then I thought: "I don't want to blow up a bank! I don't want to do anything horrible like that." I don't believe any right-minded person, teenager or not, deliberately wants to hurt other people or their own or their family's reputation by doing things like that.

I was in a real quandary because I couldn't think of anything positive to do with my life. I did want to be a teacher and I did win a teacher's scholarship, but I was manoeuvred out of that opportunity. So, I went on to become an accountant and thus was born the worst accountant the world has ever seen. (I do hope that is an exaggeration).

Inside, I still wanted to be a teacher. Eventually the Lord brought me to a place where I became a Bible teacher. Along the way I did become a teacher of accountancy as well. So, God was able to satisfy my deep inner desire, a desire He put in my DNA, to teach. Although I was blocked in certain ways and for a number of years, eventually God, when I gave him full control of my life, bought me to that inner satisfaction. He will do the same for you. He will satisfy your life with good things.

In Romans 12:1-2, the Bible says when you put your life as a living sacrifice on the altar for Him and you renew your mind by the Word of God, He will bring you into the will of God that is good and perfect and acceptable for you. The plan of God for your life is good. It will bless you. It'll be something enjoyable. It will be acceptable to you. It's something you're going to be happy about and it's something that's absolutely perfect for you. That's what God does. He brings you into that satisfying of your deep desires with good things.

(iv) The Lord restores or makes up for what you have lost.

> *Who satisfies your desire with good things so that your youth is renewed like the eagle.*
> *Psalm 103:5b*

I'm so grateful that God can turn the clock back on anything. The first promise my wife and I ever got, came when Lynne was out in the garden. We were very new Christians – just a few weeks old in the Lord. Lynne was pottering around out there and this thought came strongly, clearly and repeatedly into her mind. "Joel. Joel. Read Joel."

Lynne thought: "What is that about?" Then she got the idea that maybe there's a book named Joel in the Bible. That's how new in the Lord we were; we just didn't know. So Lynne came inside and she opened the Bible, looked through the index and sure enough, she found a book named Joel. She started reading the book of Joel and she came across this promise (2:25): The Lord will restore the years the locust has eaten.

We had wasted years, not only in our relationship, but in other ways, including financially. Now God was telling us by His Spirit and through His Word that He would restore everything we had lost in every area of life. WOW. What a promise. What a God. Over the following years that we have walked with Him, the Lord has more than restored what we lost. He has lifted us to new heights of being blessed and being a blessing to others.

God can turn the clock back in your life. Whatever you've lost you can get back, whether it's your health or finance or happiness in relationships. Whatever you've lost or wasted, God can restore it and He wants to. Or He can give you something better in its place. Will you say Amen to Him for your own situation?

There is so much good news in these first few verses of Psalm 103. And there is so much more good news everywhere else in the Bible. God wants you to have it all. That's why He sent His Son.

Jesus got what we deserved, which was punishment; so that we could get what He deserves, which is blessing. This is the good news you should be expecting in your life and family this year and beyond. Can you say Amen? If you expect to receive these things from God, you'll receive them. If you don't expect them, you won't.

Jesus got what we deserved, which was punishment; so that we could get what He deserves, which is blessing.

What is one thing you have learned from this teaching?

What is one thing you can do to implement this teaching?

Faith Declaration:

I thank You Lord for the amazing good news in your word that is all there for me, because of what Jesus did for me. I thank You Lord for giving me victory over stress and depression, so I can live in Your peace and Joy. I thank You for wrapping me in Your love and overflowing me with Your goodness and grace. I praise You for satisfying my wants and deep desires, as well as my daily needs. I give You glory for restoring all the world, the flesh and the devil have taken from me. I speak abundant restoration over my life and family, our finances and future and our ministry, in Jesus' Name. Amen.

7
5 Steps to Forgiving Others

³² Be kind and compassionate to one another, forgiving each other, just as in Christ God forgave you.
Ephesians 4:32

The New Testament clearly teaches in a number of places that forgiving others is not an option for Christians. It is essential. It is essential, not only so that we can be obedient to God, but also for our own inner health, peace and happiness. Refusing to forgive others can hurt our physical, relational and even financial well-being, as well as our spiritual health and relationship with God. Never forget that Jesus said God measures our love by our obedience. (John 14:21).

For some people, forgiveness comes easy. For others, it can be a very difficult thing; it can be something that takes time and is more of a process than an event.

In this chapter and the next, I will explain some of the steps that can help you to forgive others and to subsequently receive the holistic benefits that ensue because you have obeyed and pleased God.

(i)   Ask God to make you willing to forgive.

You have to accept that forgiveness is always about pardoning the guilty, not the innocent.

It helps you to forgive when you realise that people did not intend to hurt you. I was able to forgive my parents and others based on the attitude and prayer of Jesus: *"Father forgive them for they know not what they do."* (Luke 23:34).

My parents did not deliberately hurt me. In fact they did the best they could, given their backgrounds and lack of parental training and support such as modern society affords. However, I felt hurt and knew I needed to forgive them.

(ii)   Forgive by faith.

We forgive by faith, because we know it's the right thing to do in the sight of God and it's the right thing to do for our own inner health.

Forgiveness is a choice. We forgive others by faith, not by emotions. Forgiving those who offend us is never easy; but it is a choice we can and should, indeed we must, make. Don't say you can't, when the reality is you won't.

Jesus challenges and empowers us to love our critics, wrong-doers and even our enemies. (Luke 6:35-36). Unfortunately there may be occasions when someone really is deliberately trying to hurt us. Their intentions do not change the Word of God about forgiveness. The Lord always gives us the ability to live according to His Word and example.

In my life, when I have been majorly hurt in a single instance or wrongly-done-by in ongoing ways, I have had to keep on forgiving way beyond the 70 times 7 that Jesus recommended. (Matthew 18:21-22). Over a lifetime, for some people, it might be 70 times 70 times 70. That's around 1,000 times a year, or 20 times a week. How does that statistic compare with the reality of your life?

I acknowledge that some people live in awful circumstances of life, in which forgiveness is required almost at epidemic levels. For them I pray, and ask you to join me, that the Lord rescues them out of such situations and leads them into His good plan for their lives.

If your life is more ordinary, then, I suggest that if you had a thicker skin and didn't take offence so easily, you would have a lot less forgiving to do. Selah.

I have learned to get tough about what comes against me and stay tender in terms of what comes out of me. As I got more mature and more like Jesus (I still have a long way to go), I discovered I had less difficulty with forgiveness. I took less offence. Forgiveness became a natural and mostly easy way of life.

There are some offences that are so hurtful, so serious and so deep that you will have to forgive the person for that one offence many, many times, until it and he or she has no more power over you, over your thoughts and over your feelings.

I learned to forgive such offences and the offender(s) every time the memory came into my mind, until I was healed. I also learned how to accelerate my own inner healing process. Whenever I forgave, I would ask God for and by faith receive my healing and pray a sincere blessing upon my critic, opponent or betrayer.

(iii)   Repent of your own bad attitudes and of any part you may have played in the offence happening.

When relationships break down it is rarely ever 90% one person's fault. Many times it might be 60/40 or 70/30.

I love this contrast: Justice is when we get what we deserve. Mercy is when we do not get what we deserve. Grace is when we get what we do not deserve.

Christians must beware of wanting mercy for ourselves, but judgement and justice for others.

Don't justify your unforgiveness, your pride or your wounded ego. Remember two things: (a) You are a sinner too. You have hurt other people. (b) The Scripture warns us about God's attitude toward pride.

> ...(God) gives us more grace. That is why Scripture says: "God opposes the proud but shows favour to the humble.
>
> James 4:6

I think most of us know that if we refuse to forgive others then God will not forgive us

> Forgive us our debts, as we also have forgiven our debtors. For if you forgive men when they sin against you, our heavenly Father will also forgive you. But if you do not forgive men their sins, your Father will not forgive your sins."
>
> Matthew 6:12, 14-15

Jesus gave us a very graphic example of what the severe consequences of stubborn unforgiveness would look like in the Parable of the Unmerciful Servant. (Matthew 18:21-35).

The other thing you need to consider is that unforgiveness allows Satan access into your life to build strongholds from which he can exert controlling influences in your life.

I like to express it this way: Sin lets the devil in. This is why Holy Spirit gave us the following instruction:

> *"... do not give the devil a foothold"*
> *Ephesians 4:27*

If you give the devil a foothold, he will turn it into a stronghold in your life.

If you give the devil a foothold, he will turn it into a stronghold in your life.

There is another reason why we should forgive Christian people who offend us. In the Damascus Road experience in which Paul met the Lord, Jesus said that Paul's persecution was hurting Him. (Acts 9:4-5). Jesus feels the pain of His people. When Christians hurt, whether offender or offendee, Jesus hurts.

Not only that, but we also negatively impact another divine member of the Holy Trinity, namely, Holy Spirit. Ephesians 4:25-32 tells us that He is grieved and therefore quenched by things like unforgiveness and anger that are caused by offences and disputes.

Here is just one specific example of how disunity affects us spiritually.

In the same way you married men should live considerately with [your wives], with an intelligent recognition [of the marriage relation], honouring the woman as [physically] the weaker, but [realising that you] are joint heirs of the grace (God's unmerited favour) of life, in order that your prayers may not be hindered and cut off. [Otherwise you cannot pray effectively.]

1 Peter 3:7 AMP

(iv)   Ask God to heal you and keep on asking and praising until you are healed.

Cast your cares on the Lord, because He cares for you.

1 Peter 5:7

The LORD is close to the broken-hearted and saves those who are crushed in spirit.

Psalm 34:18

Sometimes you might write out your feelings, but send the letter to God, not to the person. The prayer ministry of journaling is such a blessing. I felt that my cares were melting away as I wrote, much more than just by saying my prayer to God. It was as if my stress levels went down as the ink flowed out of my pen.

There comes a time when you need to accept your healing by faith and then act in faith by not thinking about it, and not talking about it. This may be the first time you pray or it could be later than that, depending on how serious the wound is.

Don't wait for an apology in order to get healed. Some apologies never come. I recall once that I virtually begged for an apology from another Christian that I did not receive. I just had to learn how to forgive and be healed without it.

I cannot control the response of the people who have hurt me. Neither can you. Even when you do the right thing, there is no guarantee anyone else will also do what is right according to the Word of God. You can't even guarantee that other Christians will follow the principles of the Word.

(v) Beware of the destructive side-effects of unforgivemess

Protect yourself and others from the destructiveness that unforgiveness works in your own life and through you to others, who catch the virus of your pain and prejudice.

> *See to it that no one misses the grace of God and that no bitter root grows up to cause trouble and defile many.*
> *Hebrews 12:15*

If you do not deal with the pain you feel, it festers like an inner poison. The more you think about it, the more you re-create the pain you feel and the more negative and self-pitying you get inside. You can become judgmental, angry, resentful, revengeful or seriously depressed.

Resentment and bitterness, the fruits of unforgiveness, act together as prison bars for your soul. They limit you relationally, emotionally and spiritually. They prevent you from functioning to your best potential or ability.

To get control of your feelings, you have to get control of your thoughts. If you need help to achieve this ask for it. Ask qualified, positive, Christian people. Make yourself accountable for getting healed.

Hurt people hurt themselves. A person can make himself physically sick by constantly focusing on negatives. Eventually other people start avoiding those who are too consistently negative. That means loneliness and rejection get added on to their pain.

If you go on unhealed, you start blaming God, along with the person who offended you in the first place. Where is your spiritual strength then? Where is your faith, joy, peace and love? Who spends time with God when they are blaming Him for their problems? Who believes God is their answer, when they treat the Lord as if He was their problem?

The other thing is that hurt people hurt people. Even though you started as the victim, you are now multiplying the negativity, especially by your tongue. When people are hurt or angry, they can say things that make the situation worse, things they later regret. Effectively they are putting petrol on fire, instead of water. They are spreading the dis-ease.

What is one thing you have learned from this teaching?

_____

What is one thing you can do to implement this teaching?

_____

Faith Declaration:

I thank You Lord for sending Jesus to forgive and save me when I was an undeserving sinner. I praise You because just as You enabled Jesus to willingly go to the cross, so You are giving me the willingness to forgive all who have hurt or offended me. Lord I do this now by faith. I repent of my part in the problem and declare You are my Problem Solver and my Healer. Hallelujah. I ask You for healing and the prevention of further hurt. I declare that there will be peace, reconciliation, unity and blessing, in Jesus' Name. Amen.

Good News: Faith Food Snack Pack

8
5 More Steps to **Forgiving Others**

Bear with each other and forgive one another if any of you has a grievance against someone. Forgive as the Lord forgave you.
Colossians 3:13

Understanding that, in Luke 17:1, Jesus said offences were inevitable, we Christians must know how to overcome them. Forgiveness is a most important component of getting that victory and the healing and peace that come with it.

Jesus included in His statement *"woe to anyone through whom they come."* So, we Christians had better be careful to not cause offence or temptation to others.

This chapter outlines the second group of five ways by which we can forgive, be healed of our hurts and go forward with our life and destiny. These five ways are additional to the previous five, not alternatives to them.

(i)   Ask God to help you see things from the other person's point of view. (Philippians 2:4).

This is neither easy, nor automatic to do. It is something you have to choose to do. It is the key point of Jesus' parable of the speck in the other person's eye and the log in our own. (Matthew 7:1-3-5).

Once you can see things from the other person's perspective, it will probably lessen the negativity you felt. You might be more aware of their pain that caused them to lash out at or snub you or put you down.

Regardless of what motivated their behaviour, as Christians we should still operate according to the Golden Rule.

> *Do to others as you would have them do to you*
> *Luke 6:31*

Paul gave some great advice in his letter to the Romans.

> [17] *Do not repay anyone evil for evil. Be careful to do what is right in the eyes of everyone.* [18] *If it is possible, as far as it depends on you, live at peace with everyone.* [19] *Do not take revenge, my dear friends, but leave room for God's wrath, for it is written: "It is mine to avenge; I will repay," says the Lord.* [20] *On the contrary: "If your enemy is hungry,*

5 More Steps to Forgiving Others

feed him; if he is thirsty, give him something to drink. In doing this, you will heap burning coals on his head." 21 Do not be overcome by evil, but overcome evil with good.

Romans 12:17-21

(ii)   Ask The Lord to strengthen your resistance to offences.

Some people are way too sensitive. They make mountains out of ant-hills. They take far too long to overcome negative events or hurtful words. You must accept that offences are inevitable and unavoidable.

Life is not all about "me".

Some people are way too sensitive. Life is not all about "me"

Jesus said that in this world we would have tribulation, but to not worry about that because He had won the victory and He has given us the means to be victorious. (John 16:33; 1 John 5:4). Jesus also said that just as the world and religious leaders persecuted Him, so they would mistreat us, His followers. (John 15:18-21). So the real question is not "why me", but "why not me?"

We really do have to learn how to turn the other cheek without becoming somebody's doormat or victim. We even have to do this within our own family situations. Sometimes you have to raise your teenagers with one blind eye and one deaf ear. In other words, don't react and certainly do not overreact to absolutely everything they say and do that you might consider provocative.

Professional sportspeople and politicians have to learn to ignore criticism and not be angry with their critics, nor allow criticism to damage their performance or their confidence.

One of the important lessons I have taught people is this: divorce your opinion from your ego.

If people disagree with you, it's not an attack on you as a person. They just have a different opinion as to what is the best kind of music to play on the car radio or what is the best colour paint for the office. Even if it is concerning a matter you deem to be serious, you can still disagree without becoming disagreeable.

Our goal should be to give no offence (2 Corinthians 6:3) and take no offence (Proverbs 19:11), unless we are giving the Gospel, which by nature is offensive to some sinners.

Learn to lift up your shield of faith against offences touching your heart. Learn to wear the helmet of salvation to protect your thought life. Take control of your own mind, thoughts and emotions.

Switch your mind off the person and the problem. Think about other people and other things, not always spiritual things, but things that make you happy, that boost your faith.

> *Finally, brothers, whatever is true, whatever is noble, whatever is right, whatever is pure, whatever is lovely, whatever is admirable – if anything is excellent or praiseworthy – think about such things.*
> *Philippians 4:8*

Don't mope around, getting gloomy. Get out and do something enjoyable with someone. Talk to someone about how you are feeling. There is an old saying: "A burden shared is a burden halved." The person who first said that must have read Galatians 6:2.

(iii)   Ask God sincerely, to really bless the guilty people.

I discovered that with my deep wounds, I did not get fully and permanently healed unless and until I had done this.

We know God looks upon the heart. That is not just the other person's heart but ours as well. I remember a time when I felt I was a victim. I asked God to deal with the person who was making my life a misery. I wanted God to change him or my circumstances, so I could get away from the consistent bombardment of negativity.

You can imagine how surprised I was when the Lord said to me something like this: "Your attitude stinks. Until you stop judging him and leave him to Me and let Me fix you, I won't be changing your situation at all."

I felt I was the victim, but the Lord said to me: Your attitude stinks. I won't change your situation until you let Me fix you

---

You must develop the heart of God for others, even your enemies. Your forgiveness must be sincere, "from your heart." (Matthew 18:35).

Sincerely blessing those who have hurt me is the greatest key to healing that the Lord has revealed to me.

Sincerely blessing those who have hurt me is the greatest key to healing that the Lord has revealed to me.

You know you are healed when there is no revenge in your heart or mind, even if you were given the opportunity to take revenge. Joseph did not take revenge on his brothers, nor on General Potiphar or his manipulative wife, nor even the slave-traders who brought him to Egypt, nor anyone in the jail. David twice refused to kill Saul, when he had the king in his power. This is the heart of God. This is Christian forgiveness.

(iv)   Do only what God specifically instructs you to in regard to reconciliation

Sometimes people wonder if they should do something tangible to express their forgiveness of the other person. I do not advise that unless and until you get a clear and confirmed (by another wise Christian) witness about exactly what you should do. There are reasons for this. Firstly, the other person may not even know they have offended you in the first place. I think we all recognise the stupidity of going up to someone and saying: "I didn't like you before, but now I think you're not so bad." Expressing forgiveness to someone for an unknown offence is just a recipe for more heartache.

Secondly, the other person may not receive well, even a good thing that you do. Without judging the other person in your situation, I have known cases where such gestures were like casting pearls before swine – they were not appreciated. According to Philippians 1:9b, discernment is needed even about doing something nice for the other person.

Think about what Paul quoted from Proverbs 25:21-22 to the Romans. He says your good deed will have an impact like that of pouring hot coals on their head. Would you classify that as a pleasant experience? Will they? So, will it produce a positive response? It may better to leave things with God until the reconciliation is complete. Then wait for an occasion like an anniversary to bless the other person if you wish.

I have learned the hard way that it is best to not write things in a letter or email or text message. Words alone do not convey feelings. They can be too blunt. The other person can read a meaning into them that you never intended. If you feel you absolutely must write something (against my advice), let someone else who is uninvolved read it before you send it.

Some might ask: "Can coffee ever be wrong?" Perhaps not, but it is probably best to leave the coffee as purely a friendship time, not a problem-solving exercise. You might even say when you phone to make the date: "Can we just chat and not talk about anything serious?"

(v)   Be a Reconciler (2 Corinthians 5:18-19) and Peacemaker (Matthew 5:9).

Do all that you can to live in peace with everyone.
Romans 12:18 NLT

Of course, there are times when you simply must follow proper conflict resolution and grievance procedures. I don't have time to go into that in this book, but please, especially in church life, use Matthew 18:15-17 as your guide and God's restorative love as your motivation.

Do not let the devil use the offence or hurt or dispute to bring division in the church or disrepute to the Lord and the church in the world. Don't let the problem or issue become an emotional football or time-bomb that divides people into the "our" or "their" camp.

Yes, we have the right and responsibility to receive comfort and advice, but two wrongs don't make a right. If you just want to gossip about (often disguised in the name of a "prayer request") and criticize the person behind their back, then you are doing more damage than what the problem was in the first place. False perceptions and accusations destroy people's lives.

The opposite of reconciliation is stress between people, unhappy emotions, distorted or disrupted communication and things like that. How much better is the Lord's healing, unity and peace. Just look at the rewards such unity brings, as recorded in Psalm 133.

What is one thing you have learned from this teaching?

_____

What is one thing you can do to implement this teaching?

_____

Faith Declaration:

I thank You Lord for enabling me to see and do things as You do. I thank You for causing me to be tough concerning what comes against me and tender regarding what flows out of me. In Jesus' Name, I declare I am wearing the helmet of salvation to protect my thought life and I am lifting the shield of faith against every fiery dart of the world, the flesh and the devil. I decree that I am not easily hurt or offended. I speak Your blessing over those who affected me negatively and declare afresh my forgiveness of them. I thank You for my healing, which I believe is complete and permanent. I ask for wisdom in these and all other relationships and communications. I declare that I have the Mind of Christ and the Wisdom of God to guide me, by the help of Holy Spirit. I thank You Lord for the anointing of reconciliation and peacemaking on my life in Jesus' Name. Amen.

Good News: Faith Food Snack Pack

9 What Jesus did at **Easter**

When he had received the drink, Jesus said, "It is finished." With that, He bowed His head and gave up His spirit.
John 19:30

Then Jesus shouted out again, and he released his spirit.
Matthew 27:50 NLT

Easter is the greatest celebration time of the year for Christians in every nation and every generation. This is because Jesus paid the supreme sacrifice and won the greatest victory – His suffering and triumph changed everything for the better for everyone who will believe.

As Jesus was bleeding and dying on the cross for our salvation, He made some amazing statements. Jesus shouted out His smallest but supremely significant statement just before He yielded up His spirit to the Father.

TETELESTAI – Jesus' victory shout

Jesus shouted a 10-letter Greek word ("tetelestai") which is translated in John 19:30 by three (3) simple English words, namely, "it is finished".

Let me point out that Jesus did not cry out, as if in defeat, "I am finished", because He knew He would be raised from the dead on the third day. On every Easter Sunday, we celebrate His wonderful and supernatural resurrection, which is an absolutely foundational belief to our Christian faith.

Easter is not the mournful memory of the death of a loved one. It is the celebration of our Saviour and Lord, Jesus Christ, Who shouted out victoriously "'it' is finished!"

When Jesus was on that cross, He was not filled with self-pity and despair. Yes, He did cry out to His Father that He felt forsaken (Matthew 27:46), but we were on Jesus' mind. Our salvation and reconciliation to God and eternal sonship with Him were the joy that was set before Jesus that enabled Him to endure the cross, despising the shame of being crucified as a common criminal. (Hebrews 12:2).

Jesus did not cry out in self-pity or defeat. He shouted out victoriously "It is finished." The price was paid for salvation and every blessing and every promise in the Bible to become a reality in the lives of all believers.

I like the saying: "It was love, not nails, that kept Jesus on the cross." We should return His love, by demonstrating our love for him.

> *And He died for all, that those who live should no longer live for themselves but for Him Who died for them and was raised again.*
> *2 Corinthians 5:15*

Let me ask this question on your behalf: "What was the 'it' that was finished?"

We have a clue to the answer to this question in John's Gospel chapter 17 and verse 4. Jesus is praying to the Father just before He was arrested and sentenced to death.

> *I have brought You glory on earth by completing the work You gave Me to do.*
> *John 17:4*

So, what was the chief work the Father sent Jesus to Earth to do?

> *For the Son of Man came to seek and to save what was lost.*
> *Luke 19:10*

Jesus' primary purpose was to bring salvation to mankind, by reconciling the human race to God. To do this, He had to satisfy all the demands of the religious law and pay the penalty for our sins, past, present and future.

Warren Wiersbe is a pastor, author and theologian who researched this Greek word "tetelestai." He discovered that it was commonly used by people in a variety of occupations, back in Bible times.

Meaning of Tetelestai – Jewish priests

One of the duties of the Jewish Priests was to examine the animals which the people brought to offer to God either as sacrifices for their sins or as thanksgiving for His blessing. Their religious laws disallowed any animals that were blemished in any way.

> *[6] "A son honors his father, and a servant his master. If I am a father, where is the honor due Me? If I am a master, where is the respect due Me?" says the Lord Almighty.*
>
> *[8] "When you bring blind animals for sacrifice, is that not wrong? When you sacrifice crippled or diseased animals, is that not wrong? Try offering them to your governor? Would he be pleased with you? Would he accept you?" says the Lord Almighty.*
>
> *[13] "When you bring injured, crippled or diseased animals and offer them as sacrifices, should I accept them from your hands?" says the Lord. [14] "Cursed is the cheat who has an acceptable male in his flock and vows to give it, but then sacrifices a blemished animal to the Lord. For I am a great king," says the Lord Almighty, "and My Name is to be feared among the nations."*
>
> *Malachi 1:6a, 8, 13b, 14*

After the priest had examined their sacrifice, he would say (the Hebrew or Aramaic equivalent of the Greek word Tetelestai): "It is perfect"… "it is finished" … "it is complete." In other words, it's all there, nothing is missing, the animal is suitably unblemished for the sacrifice.

Jesus Christ, who died on the Cross for us was God's perfect, unblemished, sinless, faultless sacrifice. John the Baptist called Him *"the Lamb of God, Who takes away the sins of the world"* (John 1:29).

On the Cross, Jesus finished the work of Reconciliation, Redemption and Salvation.

Meaning of Tetelestai – Merchants

Businessmen in Jesus' day also used the equivalent of the Greek word "tetelstai." To them, it meant "the debt is fully paid." If you had purchased something, the merchant would take your money and then would give you a receipt. That receipt would say "tetelestai – it is finished." The debt has been fully paid.

As sinners, you and I are in debt to our Holy God and, like the debtors in Jesus' parable (Matthew 18:23-35), we cannot pay this debt. We have broken God's law. We are spiritually and morally bankrupt. Jesus came and paid the debt for us. That is what tetelestai means.

> *You know the Grace of our Lord Jesus Christ, that though He was rich, yet for your sake He became poor, that you through His poverty might become rich.*
> *2 Corinthians 8:9*

> *For even the Son of Man did not come to be served, but to serve, and to give his life as a ransom for many.*
> *Mark 10:45*

> *For there is one God and one mediator between God and men, the man Christ Jesus, who gave himself as a ransom for all men.*
> *1 Timothy 2:5,6*

Jesus ransomed us. He paid our Spiritual and Moral Debt in full. He became poor for us so that we could become spiritually and morally rich in the sight of God through Him.

Praise God, we were kidnapped by the devil through our sin and the Lord paid the ransom for us to be forgiven and set free.

Praise God, we committed spiritual crimes, but Jesus paid the fine that was accepted by the court of Heaven.

Jesus is the Perfect Sacrifice Who was punished for our sins so that we could experience God's loving Mercy and Grace instead of His Holy Judgment.

Jesus got what we deserved, which was punishment, so we could get what He deserves, which is blessing.

A famous Bible teacher and pastor from the 17th century, Matthew Henry, wrote a 6-volume verse-by-verse commentary on the entire Bible. In it he wrote that the death and triumph of Jesus purchased 4 things: i. Full satisfaction for sin; ii. Fatal blow to Satan; iii. Fountain of Grace that will flow forever; iv. Foundation of Peace that will last forever.

Meaning of Tetelestai – Artists

According to Warren Weirsbe, a third group of people who used the expression "tetelestai" was artists.

When a painter had put the final touches on his work, he would step back and say: "Tetelestai – it is finished!" He meant: "My picture is completed."

In other words, the concept the artist had in his mind when he began the painting was now a reality on canvas for all to see.

The Old Testament is full of prophecies about, and symbols of, the Plan and Purposes of God. They described the plan of salvation that God had in mind and which Jesus fulfilled. Two well-known examples are: (a) the sacrificial offering of his son Isaac by Abraham – Jesus was God's Son, who was sacrificed for the forgiveness of our sins; and (b) the prophetic act of Moses striking the Rock to release life-giving water for the people of God. Jesus was struck through His suffering and death on the Cross, so that believers could find new life in Him.

The first prophecy of Jesus and what He would do occurred right back in the Garden of Eden, after the sin of Adam and Eve. God said to the devil, the Offspring of the woman "...will crush your head and you will strike His heel". (Genesis 3:15). Jesus fulfilled this prophecy.

In the last twenty-four hours of His life, Jesus fulfilled 16 Messianic prophecies. Some of those prophecies were: He would be betrayed by a friend; the betrayal price would be thirty pieces of silver; He would be silent before His accusers; He would be crucified with criminals and yet buried in a rich man's tomb; He would be scourged and His body pierced, but none of His bones would be broken; His executioners would cast lots for His clothing.

Various authors, including Herbert Lockyer, have written that the mathematical possibilities of one man fulfilling each and every one of these prophecies in any time frame, or of the fulfillment being a co-incidence, happenstance or an accident are 1 in 537 million (537,000,000)

Arthur T. Pierson used an illustration similar to this: It would be as likely as if a single drop of water in the ocean was coloured bright red and a blind-folded child with a bucket was taken out to a random spot and drew out sea-water that included the only drop of red water in the entire ocean.

Another author quoted a scientist, Peter Stoner, as suggesting that the possibility of just 8 prophecies being fulfilled by Jesus were 1 in a hundred thousand million million (100,000,000,000,000,000). This would be similar to covering the entire land area of Australia with our large silver 50-cent pieces stacked 10-15 coins high. Imagine one of those coins was dyed red and submerged somewhere in that ridiculously impossible-to-count stack of coins. What would be the possibility that a prospector, with just one plunge of his arm anywhere in Australia, grasped hold of that exact red coin?

It is mathematically impossible for the prophecies Jesus fulfilled to be coincidental. He supernaturally fulfilled the previously declared Word and Will of God. Therefore mathematics proves that God is God, that the Bible is true and that Jesus is Lord.

It is mathematically impossible for the prophecies Jesus fulfilled to be coincidental. He supernaturally fulfilled the previously declared Word and Will of God. Therefore mathematics proves that God is God, that the Bible is true and that Jesus is Lord.

Meaning of Tetelestai – Victory in Battle

Author Malcolm Smith discovered a fourth use of the word "tetelestai." It was shouted by a Roman general when he saw that the enemy had been defeated.

> When you were dead in your sins and in the uncircumcision of your flesh, God made you alive with Christ. He forgave us all our sins, [14] having cancelled the charge of our legal indebtedness, which stood against us and condemned us; He has taken it away, nailing it to the cross. [15] And having disarmed the powers and authorities, He made a public spectacle of them, triumphing over them by the cross.
>
> Colossians 2:13-15

> He who does what is sinful is of the devil, because the devil has been sinning from the beginning. The reason the Son of God appeared was to destroy the devil's work.
>
> 1 John 3:8

So, Jesus came to destroy the power of sin and to set people free from the grip of the devil and from every form of darkness, evil and negativity in their lives.

The thief comes only to steal and kill and destroy; I have come that they may have life, and have it to the full.

John 10:10

Just as you and I have our own natures, it is the nature of God to love, to do good, to heal and to forgive. That's just the way He is. It is the nature of the devil to do harm and evil.

God loves people. Conversely, the devil hates people because we are made in the image of God, even if it is an image damaged by sin. A dirty, wrinkled, even torn $20 dollar note is still recognizable and valued as a $20 dollar note.

I'm reminded of the story about the scorpion and the turtle. The scorpion wanted to cross the river, but he couldn't swim. So he asked the turtle for a ride. But the turtle said, "Oh no. I can't take you on my back because if I do, you'll sting me." And the scorpion replied, "Oh no. I give you my word. I won't sting you."

The turtle, with some persuasion, finally agreed and let the scorpion get on his back.

They set out across the river together and when they had reached about the middle, the scorpion could resist no longer.

He reached underneath the shell and stung the turtle. As they began to slowly sink to the bottom, the turtle cried out: "But you promised; you promised you wouldn't sting me."

The Scorpion replied, "Yes, I know I promised. But I couldn't resist. You see, it's my nature to sting."

It's God's nature to love, to forgive, to give, to bless, to help, to heal and to empower. It's the devil's nature to hate, to accuse & offend, to steal, to curse, to hinder, to hurt and to destroy. The devil uses things such as sickness, strife and discouragement; but, sin is his chief weapon, his deadliest sting.

It was only by the sacrificing of His own sinless and wholly positive life that Jesus could make salvation available to us, in spirit, soul, body and quality of life.

You must have the confidence that Jesus has paid the price which purchased every blessing you will every need in any and every area of your life. This is what 2 Corinthians 1:20 means! Jesus said "yes" to every promise in the Bible, whether it is for salvation, reconciliation to God and man, healing, renewal of your mind, financial blessing, career advancement, leadership influence in the seven so-called mountains of society (Family, Church, Government, Education, Business, Media, Arts/Sport/Entertainment). So, healing belongs to you. Promotion belongs to you. Spiritual gifts belong to you ... all because of Jesus! Hallelujah.

The other area in which you must exercise faith is by taking up your authority in Christ to defeat the devil in your own life and family and to destroy his works in others as you minister to them in the Lord's Name.

> *Behold! I have given you authority and power to trample upon serpents and scorpions, and [physical and mental strength and ability] over all the power that the enemy [possesses]; and nothing shall in any way harm you.*
> *Luke 19:10 AMP*

By faith accept that Jesus has paid the price for every blessing and every promise in the Bible to become a reality in and through your life ... and that you have His delegated authority and power to be victorious in every area of your life

---

By faith accept that Jesus has paid the price for every blessing and every promise in the Bible to become a reality in and through your life ... and that you have His delegated authority and power to be victorious in every area of your life

---

Conclusion – 6 things that ended and 6 things that started at Easter

There is not room in this chapter to explain the following six things that Jesus finished on the Cross and the accompanying six things that started with Jesus' resurrection.

(i) It was the end of the God-ordained suffering that Jesus went through on our behalf. And it was the end of His human life, not His humanity, and the end of His laying aside His Deity.

It was the beginning of Jesus' Eternal High Priestly ministry that gives us such confidence, even boldness, before the throne of Grace. Jesus once again took up His place of glorified Lordship at the Father's right hand to speak and act on our behalf.

(ii)   It was the end of the dominating power of sin in the lives of believers.

It was the beginning of the power of inner righteousness that God would supply to every Christian through Jesus Christ.

The wonderful truth of the Gospel is that Jesus does not just set us free from the penalty of sin, He releases us from the power of sin, including pornography and other addictions such as alcohol and drugs, which induce so much sin, because people hand over the control of their lives to these negative forces.

(iii)   It was the end of the Law and of salvation through obedient, good and religious works.

It was the beginning of both salvation by grace through faith and the Age of New Covenant Grace, which ushered in times of experiencing the limitless unmerited favour and miracle-working enabling power of God, until Jesus comes again to take believers into eternity with Himself.

(iv) It was the end of all the sacrifices and religious rituals whereby man tried to get close to God, to communicate with Him and please Him by religious performances.

It was the beginning of restored relationship with God on a personal basis in which we can each and all experience God, and His Love, so that we fellowship with Him, love, honour, serve and please Him, by faith in Christ and through the power of Holy Spirit.

(v) It was the end of Israel being the primary focus of God's attention.

It was the beginning of the Christian Church taking up their inheritance as the spiritual people of God.

(vi) It was the end of Jesus in His Humanity being able to do the Father's work only in one place, at one time.

It was the beginning of the Age of Holy Spirit, Who would empower a world-wide, world-changing movement of Christian believers who do God's work and continue Christ's ministry on the earth by faith, in His power.

3 questions

In response to what you have read in this chapter: (a) Will you ask God NOW to forgive your sins? (b) Will you thank Jesus for what He did for you? (c) Will you ask the Lord for His power to be evident in your life?

What is one thing you have learned from this teaching?

_____

What is one thing you can do to implement this teaching?

_____

Faith Declaration:

I thank You Lord Jesus for taking the punishment for my sins on the Cross. I praise You for rising in triumph over sin, death and the devil. I glorify You for passing Your power, authority and victory on to me, both for myself and my needs and also to minister to others to meet their needs. I declare that I am righteous in the sight of God because of the shedding of Jesus' Blood for me. Therefore the Lord is always ready, willing and able to bless, empower and use me for His glory. I thank you that I am free from the requirements of the Law and from the effort of trying to win the approval of God by my religious performance. I praise You Lord that the curtain in the temple was torn to indicate that I have free access to My Father in Heaven, both to build our relationship and partnership, and to have my prayers answered at the Throne of Grace. I give You praise my God, because You have a limitless supply of un-earned, un-merited grace and enabling power to pour into and through my life. Hallelujah.

ABOUT THE AUTHOR

Nick Watson has been happily married to Lynne since 1970. They have 3 children, Kylie, Simon and Rebekah; 4 (so far) grandchildren Katie, Rennick, Craig and Aiden; and 1 great-granddaughter, Riley.

Nick is the Founder, Principal Prophet, Author and Teacher, and People Builder of Prophetic Power Ministries.

He was for years the Senior Pastor of Bayside Christian Family (Apostolic) Church, a thriving Spirit-filled church in Brisbane, Queensland. Australia.

Nick has been a recognised prophet in the Apostolic Church Australia for more than 25 years. He has served in various denominational leadership roles.

Nick has preached and prophesied throughout Australia and overseas, with a signs-following ministry.

YOUR FEEDBACK

If this book "Good News Faith Food Snack Pack" has encouraged your faith, please share your testimony with us at the email address below.

CONTACT Nick Watson

If you desire to contact Nick concerning a ministry engagement at your church, group, camp or leaders event please visit our website:

www.youcanprophesy.com

 www.facebook.com/nickjwatson.ycp

Gmail
email: youcanprophesy@gmail.com

OTHER BOOKS by Nick Watson

Faith Food Snack Pack – Overcoming

Faith Food Snack Pack – Healthy Soul

Faith Food Snack Pack – Holy Spirit

Lessons From My Dog – 33 Faith Lifters

You Can Prophesy – Supernatural. Simple. Safe.

Printed by Libri Plureos GmbH in Hamburg, Germany